TWELVE
FAMOUS
EVANGELISTS

by

JAMES STEPHEN

AMBASSADOR

BELFAST, NORTHERN IRELAND
GREENVILLE, SOUTH CAROLINA

Twelve Famous Evangelists
This edition 2004

ISBN 1 84030 153 8

Ambassador Publications
a division of
Ambassador Productions Ltd.
Providence House
Ardenlee Street,
Belfast,
BT6 8QJ
Northern Ireland
www.ambassador-productions.com

Emerald House
427 Wade Hampton Blvd.
Greenville
SC 29609, USA
www.emeraldhouse.com

Contents

TWELVE
FAMOUS EVANGELISTS

CHAPTER I

John Wesley

THE TRAVELLING EVANGELIST

IT is fitting that this series should be opened
by attempting, in part, to re-tell the story
of JOHN WESLEY, who was a man greatly
used of God in the preaching of the Word.
Accordingly we mention a few facts concerning
his life.

John Wesley was born on June 17th, 1703,
at Epworth, in North Lincolnshire, where
his father was the rector of the parish. Whilst
not ignoring the influence of his father along
certain lines, all his biographers are agreed
that John Wesley owed a great deal to his
mother. In fact, it has been said that she
"takes rank with the most celebrated mothers
that history recalls." It may suffice to say
of her that "she was an admirable woman,
of highly improved mind, and of a strong

and masculine understanding; an obedient wife, an exemplary mother, a fervent Christian. Her consummate management of her numerous household, her patient endurance of the pinch of poverty, her unflinching courage in the midst of trouble and danger, her deep concern for the spiritual welfare of her fellow-parishioners, her devotion to her able but somewhat erratic husband, her orderliness, reasonableness, steadfastness of purpose, calm authority, and tender affection" are some of the characteristics displayed in her life, and afterwards reflected in her son.

It will be of special interest to all University men and women to learn that in 1729 John Wesley with other kindred spirits met together several evenings in the week to read the Greek Testament. These were all members of the Church of England, and their one desire and design was to be downright Bible Christians.

This gathering became known as the "Holy Club," but the members were undaunted, and held on their way. Moreover, they sought to find ways and means of doing good unto others, and so they were frequently found engaged in errands of mercy.

In October, 1735, John Wesley, then in the thirty-third year of his age, took boat from Gravesend in order to embark for Georgia under the sanction of the Society for the Propagation of the Gospel in Foreign Parts. He returned to England in February, 1738.

This trip was more profitable to John Wesley than it was to others, but into certain aspects of this period we must not now enter. The chief lesson he learned was this, that "I, who went to America to convert others, was myself never converted to God!" The journey had brought him into touch with some Moravians, and their earnest talks began to cause him searchings of heart.

Upon his return to London he conversed with PETER BOHLER, a Moravian, and as a result of these conversations, coupled with the searching of the Scriptures and the exercise of prayer, he was led to believe on the Lord Jesus Christ, and to recognise that by faith he was not only saved, but justified, finding out the meaning of joy and peace in simply believing. And then his preaching was changed, while his utterances became the burning words of a living and rejoicing man.

It is interesting to read this account of the early days of Methodism, written by Wesley: "On Monday, May 1st, 1738, our little society began in London. But, it may be observed, the first rise of Methodism, so called, was in November, 1729, when four of us met

together in Oxford ; the second was at Savannah,
in April, 1736, when twenty or thirty persons
met at my house; the last was in London,
and on this day, forty or fifty of us agreed
to meet together every Wednesday evening,
in order to have a free conversation, begun and
ended with singing and prayer. In all our
steps we were greatly assisted by the advice
and exhortations of Peter Bohler, an excellent
young man, belonging to the society commonly
called Moravians. "

Then we trace John Wesley for the long
period of fifty-three years travelling on horseback all over England and Wales, visiting
Scotland and Ireland as well. No man knew
England better in his day than Wesley. His
Journal is not only a most valuable history of
his preaching experiences, but it also throws
light upon the general condition of the country.
There he was—a man on fire for God, looking
out upon the world as his parish, studying
as he rode, preaching in season and out of
season. Again he is revisiting and teaching
the converts, or he is organising them into
societies. But he is always at it.

It has been said that "he paid more turnpikes
than any man who ever bestrode a beast. Eight
thousand miles was his annual record for
many a long year, during each of which years

he seldom preached less frequently than a thousand times. "

We must content ourselves with one extract from the conclusion of a sermon by Wesley on Justification by Faith: "Thou ungodly one who hearest or readest these words, thou vile, helpless, miserable sinner, I charge thee before God, the judge of all, *go straight unto Jesus* with all thy ungodliness. Take heed thou destroy not thine own soul by pleading thy righteousness more or less. Go as altogether ungodly, guilty, lost, destroyed, deserving and dropping into hell; and thus shalt thou find favour in His sight, and know that He justifieth the ungodly. As such thou shalt be brought unto the Blood of sprinkling, as an undone, helpless, doomed sinner. Thus look unto Jesus! There is the Lamb of God, who taketh away thy sins!"

In appearance Wesley was small, spare, and sinewy, perfectly proportioned, and made for activity. His features were striking—the nose somewhat aquiline, the lips firm, eyes bright and vivid, piercing, commanding, yet sympathetic.

He was a keen thinker, systematic and logical. His preaching was almost always extempore. He and his audience were in living contact and sympathy with each other, not only face to face. His exposition was transparently clear, his application direct and searching. His manner was always perfectly simple and natural; at the same time he spoke with a calm authority, a serene power, which marked him out as a preacher, unique in style and character.

John Wesley honoured the Bible, he cried down sin, he made much of Christ's death, he taught the absolute need of repentance, faith, and conversion, he exalted holiness. Having fought a good fight, he ended his course triumphantly with his last words, "THE BEST OF ALL IS, GOD IS WITH US." His body lies in the sacred earth behind Wesley Chapel, London.

Chapter II

D. L. Moody

THE PIONEER EVANGELIST

DWIGHT LYMAN MOODY was born at Northfield, U.S.A., on Feb. 5th, 1837.

The manner in which he was converted had an effect upon his own future methods. He was once asked: "Mr. Moody, what is the way to reach the masses with the Gospel? To which he characteristically replied, "Go for them!" Mr. Kimball was his Bible class teacher, and evidently young Moody had been specially laid on his heart. Accordingly he went to the shoe shop in which Moody was employed, to talk to Moody about his soul. The record is very simple—"There, in the back of that store in Boston, he gave himself and his life to Christ." Mr. Kimball went after Moody, and Moody adopted that method in a variety of ways in later life.

Moody's life has been divided into four sections, viz., (1) A Sunday School worker; (2) The organiser of a church for the people;

(3) An evangelist on both sides of the Atlantic; and (4) An educator of youth.

How much could be written about the Moody Bible Institute in Chicago and its influence for good since the days of Moody! Then we think of Northfield and its many and varied activities, but we are principally interested in this article with his work in the British Isles.

In business D. L. Moody had all the marks of a pushing and successful young man. His business life was eventually in Chicago, and while there he was very busily engaged in the service of the Lord in connection with Sunday School work. He made up his mind to save a certain amount of money, and then to go out into the Lord's work and maintain himself as long as the money lasted.

Later on, and quite suddenly, he made up his mind to visit England. His reasons for so doing were for the sake of his wife's health, and that he might meet the well-known workers, C. H. Spurgeon and George Muller. Practically unknown in England, he was asked to attend the Annual Meeting of the Sunday School Union in Exeter Hall in 1867.

It was allotted to him to move a vote of thanks to the Earl of Shaftesbury for presiding. The opening of his speech must have produced quite a sensation. From his reply it can be imagined how the chairman introduced him. Moody said: "The chairman has made two mistakes. To begin with, I'm not the 'Reverend' Mr. Moody at all. I'm plain Dwight L. Moody, a Sunday School worker. And then I'm not your 'American cousin.' By the grace of God I'm your brother, who is interested with you in our Father's work for His children."

In these, his introductory remarks in his first public address in London, we can discern several marks of the character of the man.

During that visit he went to Dublin and there met Harry Moorhouse, and, in his casual way, invited Moorhouse to visit him when in America. It was about this time that he heard these words, uttered by Henry Varley: "The world has yet to see what God will do, with, and for, and through, and in, and by, the man who is fully and wholly consecrated to Him." Moody remarked: "I will try my utmost to be that man." That proved to be the great turning point in the experience of Moody.

The meeting with Moorhouse was destined to have a great influence upon him. The story is well-known how Moorhouse, making for Chicago, reminded Moody of his invitation. He

was just then leaving home but arranged that
Moorhouse should preach in his church.   For
seven consecutive nights Moorhouse preached
with fervour from the inexhaustible text,
John 3. 16. Blessing attended this preaching.   Soon Moody returned, and was impressed
then with the need of making known the love of
God, and this altered his preaching.   Henceforth
he was to declare the love of God wherever
he went.

Yet another event was used in shaping
Moody's preaching.   On October 8th, 1871,
he preached in Chicago from the words: "What
shall I do then with Jesus which is called
Christ?" (Matt. 27. 22).

That was on a Sunday night.   At the close
of the address Moody told the people to take
the text home and think over it, and to return
the following Sunday when he would deal
with the answer.   That week the great Chicago
fire took place, his church was burned down,
and many of his audience were taken away.
Moody determined ever after to preach for
immediate results.

In June, 1872, Moody came to England in
order to learn more of the Bible from English
Bible students.   During that time he was asked
to preach in a church in North London.   This
service was very much blessed, and he con-

tinue l to preach. One or two other places were also visited.

He returned to America. Some time previously he had met Ira D. Sankey. Sankey's singing capabilities had impressed Moody, and they arrange to join forces in the work of the Gospel. In 1873 Moody and Sankey visited England and began preaching in York, moving from there to Sunderland, and then to Edinburgh, followed by Glasgow, next over to Belfast, and then to London. No one who has conversed with those who remember these stirring days will doubt that Moody was God's chosen vessel. Pages could be filled with interesting items of these great revival times.

In 1881 these two brethren paid another visit to England, commencing at Newcastle-on-Tyne, and in London there was a long and fruitful time.

It may be interesting to quote some estimates of the man by those who knew him.

JOSEPH COOK wrote: "A man of prayer, a man of the Book, a man of the soundest evangelical faith, a man of extraordinary practical sagacity, organising power, and aptness for leadership, a man of combined courage and tenderness, a man endowed by unusual powerful, but balanced, emotions with greatness of character, a man of commanding spiritual manliness, a man of remarkable business and executive talent, a man working easily with associates. "

HENRY DRUMMOND wrote: "In largeness of heart, in breadth of view, in single-eyedness and humility, in teachableness and self-obliteration, in goodness of love, none can stand beside him. "

IRA D. SANKEY said: "Amid all that has been said about what has made Mr. Moody so great a man, I want to say that one of the greatest influences of his life came from his wife. She has been the brake upon an impetuous nature, and she, more than any other living person, is responsible for his success. "

ALEXANDER STEWART was very fond of recalling his visit to Moody and Northfield, and he used aptly to sum him up as "a big chunk of humanity. "

We conclude our record of a great, good, and much loved evangelist, by quoting his last words, ere he was promoted to Glory on December 22nd, 1899—"Earth is receding and Heaven opening. God is calling me. "

CHAPTER III

George Whitefield

THE FIELD EVANGELIST

IN the old South Church, at Newburyport, Massachusetts, is the cenotaph of GEORGE WHITEFIELD, surmounted by a symbol of immortality, a flame bursting from an uncovered urn. The epitaph, which reads as follows, speaks for itself: "Born at Gloucester, England, Dec. 16th, 1714; educated at Oxford University; ordained in 1736; in a ministry of thirty-four years he crossed the Atlantic thirteen times, and preached over eighteen thousand sermons."

Like many other famous men, George Whitefield was of humble origin, and had no rich or noble connections to help him forward in the world. His mother kept the Bell Inn at Gloucester, and appears not to have prospered in business; at any rate, she never seems to have been able to do anything for Whitefield's advancement in life.

In the Life of the late King Edward VII there is an extract from a letter written by his

father in which he says, "The only use of
Oxford is that it is a place for study." How-
ever, in the case of George Whitefield, and
we are sure in other instances also, the stay in
this seat of learning "was the great turning-
point in his life." Read Whitefield's own
words: "Above all, my mind being now more
opened and enlarged, I began to read the
Holy Scriptures upon my knees, laying aside
all other books, and praying over, if possible,
every line and word. This proved meat
indeed and drink indeed to my soul. I daily
received fresh life, light, and power from
above. I got more true knowledge from
reading the Book of God in one month than
I could ever have acquired from all the writings
of men."

It is interesting to read how Whitefield
was practically forced to become a field preacher.
He had gone to Islington to preach for a
Church of England friend. It was discovered
that he had not the necessary licence for
preaching in London. Accordingly he went
outside and preached in the churchyard. "And, "
he says, "God was pleased so to assist me
in preaching, and so wonderfully to affect
the hearers, that I believe we could have
gone on singing hymns in prison. Let not
thy adversary say, 'I have thrust myself

out of their synagogues.' No; they have thrust me out. "

And so from 1739 to the year of his death, 1770, a period of thirty-one years, his life was one uniform employment. He was driven to the fields. His audiences averaged two thousand, and at times swelled to incredible size; some say, at Kingswood and in Cornwall, to ten thousand; at Philadelphia, to twenty thousand; at Boston Common, to thirty thousand; and at Moorfields, London, sixty thousand hearers.

When in England he preached a good deal in London. In 1748 he became known to the Countess of Huntingdon. This titled lady was instrumental in obtaining the services of notable preachers. She made Whitefield one of her chaplains. In a letter Whitefield wrote: "Good Lady Huntingdon is come to town and I am to preach at her Ladyship's house twice a week to the great and noble. O that some of them may be effectually called, and taste of the riches of redeeming love! About thirty have desired to come, and I suppose they will bring thirty more. I have heard of two or three more dear Christians among the great ones. I know you will pray the Lord of all lords to increase their number. "

It was largely through the liberal contributions of Lady Huntingdon and other persons of rank that Whitefield's Chapel in Tottenham Court Road was built. There he preached the message of life to large audiences.

Whitefield died in 1770 at the comparatively early age of fifty-six. The day before he died he set out on horseback to fulfil a preaching engagement. Before he spoke, a friend remarked to him, "Sir, you are more fit to go to bed than to preach." To this Whitefield replied, "True sir," and then turning aside, he clasped his hands together, and looking up, said: "Lord Jesus, I am weary in Thy work, but not of Thy work. If I have not yet finished my course, let me go and speak for Thee once more in the fields, seal Thy truth, and come home and die." The Lord granted him his desire.

It is good to recall the fact that before his death he made request that John Wesley should be asked to preach his funeral sermon. Wesley and he had long ceased to agree about Calvinistic points; but Whitefield, to the very last, was determined to forget minor differences, and to regard Wesley as Calvin did Luther, "only as a good servant of Jesus Christ."

Many unusual incidents happened during the course of his preaching. We mention one. At one of his large field gatherings, Whitefield had mounted the temporary scaffold to speak. Then he announced his text: "It is appointed unto men once to die, but after this the Judgment" (Heb. 9. 27). After a short pause, a wild, terrifying shriek issued from the centre of the congregation. Whitefield waited to ascertain the cause. Mr. Grimshaw came to him and said, "Brother Whitefield, you stand amongst the dead and dying—an immortal soul has been called into eternity—the destroying angel is passing over the congregation, cry aloud, and spare not!"

Again Whitefield announced his text, and once more there was a loud and piercing shriek. Thus another person passed from time into eternity. After the consternation had somewhat subsided, Whitefield continued. "All was hushed—not a sound was to be heard—and a stillness, like the awful stillness of death, spread itself over the assembly, as he proceeded in a strain of tremendous eloquence to warn the careless, Christless sinner to flee from the wrath to come."

There are many lessons to be learned from the life and labours of Whitefield which should be useful to all preachers. We mention three:

1. He studied the proper use of his voice. Dr. A. T. PIERSON has written thus about

Whitefield's voice: "Like his Lord before him, 'he opened his mouth and taught them.' He spoke with loud and clear tones, with perfect articulation and enunciation. His voice was a great gift, but his management of it made the perfection of the faculty of human speech. It had wonderful richness and sweetness; but behind its musical modulations and persuasive pathos there lay deep feeling. It was the man, back of the voice, that so warmed the cold, calculating Franklin, and charmed the philosophical, sceptical Hume."

2. He studied illustration. He turned incidents of the day to good use. On one occasion Lord Chesterfield was in his audience, and as Whitefield described a blind beggar stumbling over the edge of a precipice, Chesterfield was so enchanted that he cried out, "Good God! he is gone!"

3. He studied simplicity. Whitefield used the words most easily understood. He abhorred long and involved sentences. His business was to make hard things easy.

May all open-air preachers catch something of the spirit which enabled George Whitefield to serve his Lord and Master so well!

CHAPTER IV

Thomas Chalmers

THE PARISH EVANGELIST

DR. THOMAS CHALMERS was one of the most illustrious of Scotland's sons.

There were many sides to his life but we are compelled to restrict ourselves to the consideration of the evangelical aspect of his life and work.

He was born March 17th, 1780, at Anstruther, in Fifeshire. At the age of eleven he went to the St. Andrews University. In 1803 he was settling in Kilmany as the minister of that parish. As the results of a serious illness his thoughts were occupied with Wilberforce's "Practical View of Religion." This was the means of a very definite work of grace in his soul which affected his whole life.

Sir Henry Moncrieff writes of this period after referring to Wilberforce's book: "This was the torch in the hand of the Almighty to kindle the flame which began in 1811 to burn with unexpected brightness in the manse and in the parish of Kilmany. Seven years of an ineffective ministry, according to his own confession, had passed; and more intellectual light had discovered to him the value of the evidence powerfully exhibited by Bishop Butler in the celebrated *Analogy*. He had sympathised with the proofs adduced by Paley; but now the force of truth through the operation of the Holy Spirit had laid hold of the whole man. Everything was changed ; "all things had become new" (2 Cor. 5. 17). The parish church had hitherto been very thinly attended. But during the three years that followed the change, that humble tabernacle was crowded. Both the high and the low were attracted by the unwonted utterances that came from its pulpit. A great evangelist had sprung up in the quiet rural localities, whose power of rivetting men's attention, and commending Jehovah's Message, was unprecedented in the experience of more than one generation.

In 1815 Chalmers took up his great work in the Tron Church in the City of Glasgow, where he exercised a great and good influence, and many were blessed through his ministry.

Dr. Chalmers was interested in the work of missions, and in May, 1817, he preached the anniversary sermon of the London Missionary Society in London. Surrey Chapel was crowded from seven in the morning, four hours before the service began.

The children's claims were felt by Chalmers, and he inaugurated a system of Sunday Schools in the district where the people lived, and this in a day when Sunday Schools were looked upon with considerable suspicion.

After four years at the Tron Church he was appointed to the new parish of St. John's, Glasgow, which was formed especially for him, so that he might have the independence necessary to carry out the great schemes which had been forming in his mind. His idea was expressed by one as follows "To provide for the submerged of that population of 10,000 poor and labouring people subject to all the fluctuation of daily work, and those accidents which constantly convert the poor, who can just keep the wolf from the door and no more, into recipients of charity. Chalmers, for all his revenue, had the plate at the church door." This worked admirably, and the poor were thus helped by the church.

In 1823 he left Glasgow in order to find rest after the stress and strain of these years. He occupied the Chair of Moral Philosophy in St. Andrews for five years, and during that time wrote several books. One remarkable result of his work in St. Andrews was the greater number of students—among them the distinguished missionary, Dr. Duff—who devoted themselves to missionary labours in India and elsewhere.

From St. Andrews he came to Edinburgh, where he had been appointed to the chair of Divinity in the University. In Edinburgh he at once assumed his natural place as a great leader of the church, and one of the most important personages in Scotland. In addition to lecturing to his students, he was in demand as a preacher. It was Chalmers who preached on "The Expulsive Power of a New Affection."

But things were not going well in the church, and in due course Chalmers found himself as the leader of the Evangelical section.

In April and May, 1838, he delivered a series of lectures in the Hanover Square Rooms, London, on "The Establishment and Extension of National Churches." These were attended by "dukes, marquises, earls, viscounts, barons, baronets, bishops, and Members of Parliament." There he stated the principles which led to the Disruption in 1843. In his last lecture delivered before a great audience, including nine bishops of the Church of England, he said: "We own no head of the church but the Lord Jesus Christ. Whatever is done ecclesiastically is done by our ministers as acting in His name, and in perfect submission to His authority."

May 18, 1842, is one of the great dates in the history of Scotland. The General Assembly of the Established Church was due to meet. By four o'clock in the morning eager spectators had begun to fill the church. When the proceedings were opened "a rustle of movement was heard, and the well-known white head and pale, impressive, heavy countenance of Chalmers became suddenly visible, with the moderator in his robes by his side, issuing from the door: and behind him an endless line, figure after figure, appearing like an army. More than four hundred ministers walked in that line, leaving their all in this world—their incomes, their positions, their homes—behind them for ever."

Thus free from State patronage, they proceeded under different conditions; as Chalmers said: "I trust, till the light of the Gospel be carried to every cottage door within the limits of the Scottish territory." It is impossible to contemplate the immense spiritual blessing which came to Scotland through this great severance.

After returning from a course of visits in England, Chalmers was found dead in his bed on May 30th, 1874.

Considering Thomas Chalmers as a preacher, we are told that the prime factor of his preaching was his spiritual conviction. "It was not his aim to convert men to a creed, in the belief that once that creed was adopted it would mould their spirit and their lives aright. He flew directly at their souls. He plied them with the message of the Gospel, that he might bring them into vital contact with God, and kindle in them that life without which they were little better than lumps of clay. Never did a preacher devote himself more thoroughly to the great business of moving men. To produce movement was his passion; movement along evangelical lines, and always directed to a glorious consummation—the salvation of individuals and the production of a happy, prosperous, regenerated community."

His name is held in reverence wherever the Scottish tongue is spoken.

CHAPTER V

W. P. Lockhart

THE YOUNG MEN'S EVANGELIST

WILLIAM PEDDIE LOCKHART was born in Kirkcaldy on 15th October, 1835.

In this town he spent the first eleven years of his life. With the moving of his parents to the Merseyside, young Lockhart made his aquaintance with Birkenhead and Liverpool, where he was eventually to find his sphere of service.

Dr. Alexander Maclaren of Manchester, in his preface to "The Life of Lockhart," gives a brief sketch of this man and his work, from which the following is a quotation:

"Porridge and the Shorter Catechism used to be the food for growing lads in Scotch households; and each in its own way, made bone and muscle. In body and mind, Mr. Lockhart had been nourished on such diet, and both had thriven accordingly. The stalwart figure, broad-shouldered and erect, the strong face which spoke of a determined will, but with many a curve which betrayed underlying tenderness, and the twinkle of a saving sense of humour in the eye, answered well to the vigorous, resolute, and withal loveable character of the man who was at once athlete and evangelist, merchant and pastor.

He was a very unconventional Christian teacher, in days when it had not yet become conventional to be unconventional, A man who was captain of a Liverpool eleven, and vaulted over a five-barred gate outside the church where he was about to hold a revival service, was certainly not cast in the ordinary mould; and did good work in illustrating by his life the possibility of blending high animal spirits and frank enjoyment of athletic exercises with earnest religion.

"Not less remarkable and still more valuable as an object lesson to-day was the other combination of commercial pursuits, and the evangelistic and pastoral office. For thirty years or so, Mr. Lockhart carried that double weight; and, thanks to his splendid physique, and also to his earnest godliness, for the greater part of that period bore it lightly. In these days when a strong current is running in the direction of elevating the Christian ministry into a sacerdotal order, it is wholesome to have the example of such a man. He was certainly in the line of apostolic succession in pursuing his calling, and thereby proved himself heir to the fishermen and tent-makers. "

W. P. Lockhart had a definite experience of conversion. Although he knew the truth intellectually, and could have detected and refuted any error in its statement, it was not until he was twenty years of age that the good news of God's salvation came home to his own heart. He had long thought of these things, he knew his need and his danger, but it was when travelling in Wales with a cousin in 1855 that the great change took place. One day when William was walking alone by the Menai Straits near the Tubular Bridge, the words "It is finished" were flashed into his mind with as much force and distinctness as though he heard them spoken from Heaven: from that moment the great fact of Christ's death for sinners became the central thought of his life.

On 2nd February, 1859, he was baptised by Mr. H. S. Brown at Myrtle Street Chapel, and the following Sunday became a member of the Myrtle Street Baptist Church.

Liverpool's Lay Preacher was described as "a tall, powerfully built man, whose every movement and attitude recalled the day when

W. P. Lockhart was famous throughout England as the best wicket-keeper in the country, the man whose stout frame and long arms behind the wicket quietly stopped the swiftest bowling. "

Lockhart threw himself into the Y.M.C.A. Movement in the early days, but insisted on conversion to God being the sole title to full membership

When he began preaching he was twenty-five years of age. Soon his ability in this direction became manifest. His manliness made an appeal to the youth of that city. He drew up a list of rules to guide him, a few of which may be mentioned:

1. To deal more with men individually, as if I were only speaking to one person.

2. To deal with men more definitely on the ground of sins committed.

3. Refer more to Scripture, turning to passages when quoting.

4. Pray in private at least as long as I speak in public.

The preacher, with a passion for souls, soon began to take journeys for the purpose of witnessing for Christ. Naturally he returned to his native country and preached in many parts. One of his early tours was through parts of the Stewartry of Kirkcudbright.

During one visit to Scotland he was asked to settle down and take charge of the well-known Carrubbers' Close Mission. He decided to to return to the Merseyside.

Just about that time theatres and public halls were being engaged for preaching purposes. A committee of business men in Liverpool was formed to promote this work, Mr. Reginald Radcliffe and W. P. Lockhart being among the number.

In halls and in parks Lockhart would be found preaching the message of salvation. Then a more permanent form of work engaged his attention, which eventually led to the opening of Toxteth Tabernacle. The first sermon preached on the ground where the Tabernacle was erected was when C. H. Spurgeon laid the foundation stone of the new building. There was a link between Spurgeon and Lockhart, and the latter sometimes received a letter from Spurgeon like this: "Will you oblige a poor cripple and preach at the Tabernacle on Sunday?" These visits to the Tabernacle were always appreciated

He continued in business during these years; first as a merchant, and then as manager in the Liverpool Investment Building Society.

When a census was taken of the attendances at Protestant places of worship in 1881, Toxteth

Tabernacle headed the list with 1200 at the morning service.

Thus Lockhart continued in season and out of season, in all parts of the British Islands, sometimes in Spain, preaching Christ. At the same time a Church had been formed in Liverpool, with the observance of the Lord's Supper every Lord's Day, and the practice of baptism of believers by immersion. During a visit to Ballater, Aberdeenshire, after a few days' illness, this honoured servant of Christ was called home on 12th August, 1893.

The following year Dr. Maclaren of Manchester unveiled a tablet in Toxteth Tabernacle, which bears the following inscription:

"In loving memory of William Peddie Lockhart. Born, 15th October, 1835; died, 12th August, 1893. An earnest preacher of the Gospel for thirty-three years. Founder and for twenty-four years the beloved pastor, of the Church meeting in this Tabernacle, which was, mainly through his exertions, opened free from debt. He won many souls for Christ, and fed the flock of God by careful exposition of the Scriptures. A workman approved of God rightly dividing the Word of truth. His strong personality, his kindness and consistency, and his conspicuous loyalty to his Lord, secured for him the respect and affection of all his fellow-citizens. Throughout his career he maintained himself as an upright and diligent man of business. Erected in grateful remembrance of his varied gifts and faithful ministry. "

May the record of this useful and fruitful life be a means of encouragement and blessing to all those who read it.

CHAPTER VI

Charles Haddon Spurgeon

THE PASTORAL EVANGELIST

CHARLES HADDON SPURGEON was born on June 19th, 1834, ten days after WILLIAM CAREY died in India. Like John Calvin, Jonathan Edwards, Jeremy Taylor, George Whitefield, and William Tyndale, Spurgeon died when he was fifty-seven years of age.

Spurgeon was born in a quaint little cottage at Kelvedon in Essex. He was converted on January 6th, 1850. A storm prevented him reaching the place of worship whither he was bound, and instead he turned into the Primitive Methodist Chapel, Artillery Street, Colchester. The regular preacher was hindered from coming on account of the weather. An unknown preacher was asked to take the service, and his audience consisted of a dozen or fifteen people. The preacher fastened his eyes on the youth and said, "Young man you look very miserable," and then he added, "Young man, look to Jesus Christ! Look! Look! Look! You have nothing to do but look and live." Far more was accomplished by that preacher than he had any conception of at the time. Spurgeon's conversion was real.

Like many another young convert Spurgeon's earliest service was found in the distribution of tracts and later in taking a Sunday School Class. The first address delivered by him was to a little company gathered together in a cottage when he addressed them from the words, "Unto you that believe He is precious" (1 Peter 2. 7).

On December 18th, 1853, Spurgeon preached in New Park Street, London, to an audience of about eighty people. So great was the impression made that those who heard him got busy during the afternoon with the result that a much larger number listened to him in the evening. As a result, the comparatively unknown young preacher was called to the pastorate of that church, and then began his life's work in London. Very soon the accommodation in the church was too small, and it was decided to enlarge the building.

In the meantime, while the alterations were being carried out, Spurgeon broke with tradition, and from February to May, 1855, the services were held in the well-known Exeter Hall. There crowds gathered to hear the young preacher.

On Sunday evening, October 19th, 1856, the Surrey Music Hall was taken for preaching. Ten thousand persons were in the hall and another ten thousand in the gardens unable to enter. It was then an alarm of "Fire" was raised, followed by great commotion, when seven lost their lives.

On the day of National Humiliation, on account of the Indian Mutiny, Spurgeon preached in the Crystal Palace to a congregation of of 23,654 persons, counted in at the turnstiles, and up to that date the assembly was described as "the largest ever addressed by a preacher of the Gospel in Europe or the world."

In connection with the Crystal Palace service, an interesting incident is recalled. Spurgeon went to the Palace to try the acoustics of the place. Having to say something, he said something worth saying: "Behold the Lamb of God which taketh away the sin of the world" (John 1. 29). A workman busy in one of the galleries heard the words, that seemed to come to him from Heaven, and, smitten with conviction of sin, he put down his tools and went home, nor did he rest until he was able to rejoice in Christ as his Saviour.

Although the great preacher could not be induced to cross the Atlantic, he paid visits to Scotland, and certain parts of the continent of Europe. In Edinburgh he felt himself to be a failure, he thought the Spirit of God had deserted him, and he told the people that the chariot wheels had been taken off. He was subject to such moods to the end, but a confession like that shows clearly enough that at other times, in spite of his easy eloquence his reliance was on God's Spirit, and not on himself.

Remarking on his visits to different places he could bear this witness "I cannot remember visiting a single village or town that I have visited a second time, without meeting with some who praised the Lord that they had heard the Word of truth there from my lips."

Eternity alone will reveal how many people were saved in the Tabernacle. "How many thousands have been converted here!" he exclaimed at the prayer meeting on May 26th, 1890, as he looked round the building. "There has not been a single day but what I have heard of two, three, or four having been converted; and that not for one two, or three years, but for the last ten years!" Surely that is a thing unmatched in the history of the Church. The membership of the Church when he came

to it in New Park Street in 1854 was 232;
and at the end of 1891 there had been baptised
and added to the Church 14,460 others; and
the membership then stood at 5311. At
one Communion Service 100 persons were
admitted to membership and 150 at another;
the greatest number added to the membership
in any one year was 571, in 1872; in 1874
there were 509, and 510 in 1875.

He loved preaching in the open-air, and
on Sunday morning, July 28th, 1878, he
preached to a crowd of from fifteen to twenty
thousand people at Rothesay in Scotland.

It was only natural that such a well-known
man should be sought after by all kinds of
people. On one occasion a person called
at his house without an appointment, and
when refused an interview, would not take
a denial. He sent a second message that
"one of the Master's servants wanted to see
him on the Master's business." Spurgeon
sent a reply that he was very sorry, but at
that very moment he was engaged with the
Master Himself, and had no time for the
servant.

Spurgeon's sermons were printed regularly.
Considerably more than a hundred million
of the weekly sermons have been sold, and
they have been reproduced in numberless

other ways. On one occasion the publishers received an order for a million copies, on another a quarter of a million copies were bought to be distributed in volumes of twelve or more to the students in the Universities, Members of Parliament, the Crowned Heads of Europe, and the householders in Ireland.

David Livingstone carried through Africa the Sermon "Accidents not Punishments," No. 408; it was returned at length to Mr. Spurgeon with a note along the top, "Very Good. D.L.", and was treasured by the preacher. Time would fail to tell of the many activities of Spurgeon. There was his college where, at the date of his death, nearly nine hundred men had been trained for the ministry. Spurgeon's Orphanage was another aspect of his work, and remains to this day.

In the last hour of the last day of January, 1892, the spirit of Spurgeon sped Home from his loved Mentone. He was buried in London, and at the grave Archibald G. Brown, the most distinguished of Spurgeon's men, and his close friend, pronounced a eulogy, of which the following is an extract: "Beloved President, Faithful Pastor, Prince of Preachers, Brother Beloved, Dear Spurgeon—we bid thee not 'Farewell,' but only for a little while 'Good night.' Thou shalt rise soon at the first dawn of the Resurrection Day of the Redeemed. Yet is the good night not ours to bid, but thine; it is we who linger in the darkness; thou art in God's holy light. Our night shall soon be passed, and with it all our weeping. Then, with thine, our songs shall greet the morning of a day that knows no cloud nor close; for there is no night there. "

CHAPTER VII

Brownlow North

SOCIETY EVANGELIST

BROWNLOW NORTH was born on January 6th, 1810. He was the only son of Charles Augustus North, Rector of Alberstoke, Hants. His grandfather was the Hon. Dr. Brownlow North, Prelate of the Noble Order of the Garter, who was successively the Bishop of the Sees of Lichfield, Worcester, and Winchester. Mr. North was thus a grand-nephew of Lord North, the celebrated Prime Minister of George III.

Although Brownlow North was born at Winchester House, Chelsea, and married a clergyman's daughter in Ireland, Scotland was the land of his adoption; in it was the home of his choice.

He belonged to the nobility of the land and was consequently educated at Eton and Oxford. Soon he became a man about town, and lived his life after the manner of his class. The pleasures and things of this world occupied the dominating place in his life.

In the course of time we read of him visiting the godly Duchess of Gordon, at Huntly Lodge, and of that gracious lady engaging him in conversation about spiritual things.

For a little he began to think on such matters, and even came to Cheltenham to consult with his friend, Frederic Robertson, who became the well-known preacher at Brighton.

He settled in Dallas, near Forres, and it was while there he experienced a great conversion. Some years later he related his experience to the students of the Edinburgh University. These are his words: "It pleased God, in the month of of November, 1854, one night when I was sitting playing cards, to make me concerned about my soul. The instrument used was a sensation of sudden illness, which led me to think that I was going to die. I said to my son, 'I am a dead man; take me upstairs.' As soon as this was done, I threw myself down on the bed. My first thought then was: Now, what will my forty-four years of following the devices of my own heart profit me? In a few minutes I shall be in Hell, and what good will all these things do me, for which I have sold my soul? At that moment I felt constrained to pray, but it was merely the prayer of a coward, a cry for mercy.... I did pray, and though I am not what I should be, yet I am this day what I am, which at least is not what I was. I mention this because I believe that every man has in his life his turning-point."

The change was complete in this man, and he began to spend hours over his Bible, and eventually he mustered courage to give away tracts. One Sunday the minister of the church in Dallas was called away from home, and it was discovered that a preacher was not available. Brownlow North was persuaded to occupy the pulpit. Thus in the providence of God the ministry of Mr. North began at Dallas, which had been for many years the scene where he lived after the course of this world, eagerly following its fashions, frivolities, and sins.

In due course, requests to preach in other places in the North of Scotland were received, and thus the way of this servant of the Lord was being opened up. He began to travel in different parts of the country, and he availed himself of every opportunity to witness for his Lord. The Church of Scotland heard of his abilities, and it was agreed that Mr. North should be officially recognised by the church as an evangelist. This was a somewhat unusual practice. He was examined as to his beliefs, and gave the fathers of the church great satisfaction. Then at the General Assembly of the church held in Edinburgh, the Moderator, Principal Cunningham, addressing Brownlow North in the name of the Assembly, said, among many things: "I have been called, by unanimous decision of this House, to recognise and welcome you as a servant of Jesus Christ who has received unusual gifts for preaching the glad tidings of great joy, and whose work in this department the Lord has greatly honoured. I never could see the warrantableness of any Church of Christ venturing to lay down as a resolution that she would not see, and would not recognise, gifts for preaching or for the ministry, except in men who had gone through the whole of the ordinary curriculum. No church has a right to lay down that rule." Mr. Brownlow North made good use of the opportunity afforded him of thanking the Assembly and proceeded to state certain defects in the religion of that day

Brownlow North had access to the great houses of the land. When visiting Haddo House in 1862, as the result of an address, he was instrumental in leading two sons of the Earl of Aberdeen to a knowledge of Christ. We read of him being in London and preaching to large audiences in the Agricultural Hall. Then he goes on to stay with Lord Cavan, returning to town to preach for Adolph Saphir. Next we find him preaching to large crowds in Londonderry as well as holding open-air meetings. This Irish visit was about the time of the '59 Revival. Back to London, addressing young men in Exeter Hall or reaching the upper classes in London in Willis's Rooms and St. James' Hall. Sometimes he is in the company of Reginald Radcliffe as when the meetings were arranged for him in Edinburgh University. Dr. Robert Howie, of Glasgow, said: "I remember well how deeply I was impressed when as a student I heard him for the first time. He made me feel as if I were moving among unseen realities, and on each successive occasion as I listened to his appeals I derived a similar benefit to my own soul."

Brownlow North's personal appearance was one that was likely to imprint itself on the memory of all who ever heard him preach. Somewhat under middle height, he was of portly form, deep-chested, broad-shouldered; his address was gentlemanly, and his bearing aristocratic. His manner in private as well as in public was marked by dignity and gravity. Though he dressed in dark clothes, generally in black, his attire was that of a country gentleman.

He was a great doctrinal preacher. He was eloquent, but his eloquence consisted in the clear, powerful, and earnest statement, exposition, and application of the great doctrines. He had not the thrilling pictorial power of Dr. Thomas Guthrie, the marvellous fecundity of illustration and the telling musical voice of Charles Spurgeon, the telling command of simile and analogy of William Arnot, or the exhaustless fund of anecdote of D. L. Moody. His style was terse and plain, but unadorned. He had no rounded periods, no graceful similes, no oratorical peroration. Often voice and words both failed him in the climax of his most earnest appeals. His power lay in the solemn and forcible statement of his doctrine, in his convincing proof and his thrilling application of them.

The following words are inscribed on his tombstone in Edinburgh: "At the age of forty-four years he was turned from an ungodly life to serve the Lord; thereafter he preached the Gospel with singular power and was greatly honoured in winning of souls to Jesus."

Brownlow North was a chosen vessel, and

was specially fitted to witness among the upper classes. May the Lord raise up more men of this type so that persons of standing and influence might be led to a knowledge of the Lord Jesus Christ.

CHAPTER VIII

Alexander Marshall

THE ITINERANT EVANGELIST

ALEXANDER MARSHALL was born on December 13th, 1846, in Stranraer, Wigtownshire. Like many Wigtownshire lads he found his way to Glasgow, where he was employed by Messrs. Arthur & Co., for a number of years. He had promise and prospect of being a successful business man.

The consciousness of his need of a Saviour began to exercise his mind. Hearing that Mr. Gordon Forlong was preaching in a Circus in Ingram Street, Glasgow, the subject of this article decided to go to the circus one evening. Mr. Marshall's own account of the meeting must be given:

"I though he was a most extraordinary preacher. I can distinctly recollect him frequently repeating the words: 'It's the Blood that saves. It's the Blood that saves.' In showing that all that was necessary for the sinner's deliverance was completed by Christ on the Cross, he exclaimed: 'It's finished; it's finished; it's finished.'

"In thinking about salvation my mind had been occupied with 'believing' instead of with the object of faith—Christ and His finished work. I imagined I believed but not in the right way. The words, 'It is finished' were carried home by the Holy Spirit to my heart and conscience. I asked myself, 'What is it that is finished?' I remembered the words were the dying words of the Lord Jesus (John 19. 30). He explained the meaning of the wondrous statement and showed that the sacrificial work had been completed— that Christ had 'put away sin by the sacrifice of Himself' (Heb. 9. 26; John 1. 29), and that every one who believed on Him was saved, and had eternal life. Specially did he dwell on the blessed truth, that the very moment any one believed he was saved. 'He that believeth on Me hath everlasting life' (John 6. 47). I had always supposed that I must feel some great change before I could be sure I was saved, and was continually looking into my heart to find peace.

"The preacher seemed to understand my difficulties, and explained that one must first believe on Jesus—and the feelings would follow, and clinched the truth by repeating again and again the following statement: 'Believing is the root, feeling is the fruit; believing is the root, feeling is the fruit.' The light from Calvary shone in upon my soul. I saw that Jesus had died in my stead and received sin's penalty, and that through believing the 'good news' made known to me in the Word I was saved and had everlasting life."

When God saved Alexander Marshall, He called him to His service. At once there were evidences of his concern for his fellow men, and out of gratitude to the Lord for all that He had done for him, Mr. Marshall sought to win others to the same Saviour. He was an evangelist from his conversion. He had a continuous longing after the spiritual welfare of men.

All the while Alexander Marshall was daily engaged in the drapery warehouse, meriting the approval of his employers, and steadily working his way toward the position of responsibility which he ultimately occupied. Another employee of this firm was at the same time showing the same steadfast zeal in the service of Christ, Alice Todd, an enthusiast for Christ, who afterwards became Mrs. Todd Osborne, was just commencing what proved to be her life work among the soldiers in the Old Barracks in the Gallowgate, and found a ready helper in Alexander Marshall.

In the year 1874, D. L. Moody and Ira D. Sankey visited Glasgow, and a real wave of blessing passed over the city. The foundations of the evangelistic activities which are features of Glasgow's religious life to-day were laid at this time, and it was Mr. Marshall's privilege to share in that great movement. He was a valued helper in the aftermeetings, and pointed many to the Saviour. He was introduced to Mr. Moody by Dr. Morrison.

An important decision was reached in Mr. Marshall's life when he decided to devote the whole of his time to the Lord's Service. As he used to remark, leaving his business calling did not make him an evangelist. He was an evangelist while in business.

In the course of his long life of service there were few towns and districts in Great Britain that this ardent soul winner did not visit. The following testimony of Pastor D. J. Findlay, J.P., of the Tabernacle, Glasgow, is worthy of mention:

"I knew A.M. well in 1874 and onward for some years. In later years I saw little of him, but always retained a high regard for him, and from first to last we were 'Alick' and 'David' when we met.

"When Moody left Glasgow in the summer

of 1875 a committee of young men was appointed to carry on the great Young Men's Meetings. I think A. M. was one of this Committee.

"In July-September, 1874, I conducted week-end services in Dunoon, which God made a very wonderful blessing. One Sunday in July 'Alick' came to our help, and of that day we have a very vivid recollection. The afternoon was spent studying a little book, 'Trust in the Living Father,' which Henry Varley had just published. At night in a crowded church 'Alick' gave a burning message, commencing with the often used words: 'Fellow-travellers on the road to Eternity,' and with repeated appeals, 'Young man, where will you spend Eternity?' Hundreds were brought to Christ through these meetings."

Something of the spirit of Paul had taken hold of Alexander Marshall, so that he was always stretching out to other regions to proclaim Christ. Hearing of the opportunities in Canada, he sailed from Liverpool on December 24th, 1879. The Lord abundantly blessed the labours of his servant in Canada, and he was instrumental in leading many souls to the Saviour of men.

Wherever he went whether visiting Canada and the United States many times, or the West Indies, or Iceland, Shetland,

Orkney, and other islands, or New Zealand, or Russia—the one ruling object in all his life and travels was to preach Christ. He always spoke with the end in view of reaching the souls of men. His presentation of the Gospel was simple and Scriptural, and abundantly illustrated by anecdotes.

Many incidents like the following could be told regarding this evangelist and his work:

Notable among these were two series of meetings held in the town of Kilmarnock, the first in 1876, and the other in 1892. On both occasions the interest aroused was remarkable, and the numbers attending gave evidence of a real spiritual awakening. A great number made profession of faith in Christ. Most of the converts of the first mission have been removed by death. When these lines were being completed news of the Home-call of a brother in far-off Canada came to hand, and at the end of the notice appeared these words: "Saved in the Tent at Kilmarnock, under the preaching of Alexander Marshall, 52 years ago." The fruits of the second mission have enriched the spiritual life of Ayrshire and the West of Scotland. Not a few of those who are doing a notable work in the spread of the good tidings in these parts were brought to the Lord at that time. A brother, who had been for many years an ardent soul winner, wrote to Mrs. Marshall as follows: "It is now thirty-six years ago since your husband led me as a young lad of 15 years of age to Christ in the town of Kilmarnock. "

"God's Way of Salvation, " by A.M., has been distributed to tens of thousands, and through its message many have been led to Christ.   "The Herald of Salvation, " was edited by A.M., for many years, and this was likewise instrumental in bringing blessing to many.

A.M. was an indefatigable tract distributer. We have known him while attending the Keswick Convention to be up very early in morning, going round as many houses as possible and dropping tracts into the letter-boxes. He was always posting literature to all parts of the world.

Alexander Marshall was one of the most interesting and entertaining types of men to meet.   His wide knowledge of the world, his intimate acquaintance with books, his correspondence with workers in the great harvest field, and his love of a theological argument, made an hour or two in his genial company pass very quickly. He was a faithful steward with regard to all that was entrusted

to him.   He loved to speak in a good broad
Scots tongue among his friends.

He was called home on August 9th, 1928.
His death created a vacancy in the service of
the Lord, which has not been filled.   May
the memory of his long and useful and fruitful
life stir up many hearts to do, as dear A.M.
so frequently quoted:

> "Now will I tell to sinners round
> What a dear Saviour I have found;
> I'll point to Thy redeeeming blood,
> And say, 'Behold the Way to God.'"

CHAPTER IX

Duncan Matheson

THE OPEN-AIR EVANGELIST

DUNCAN MATHESON was born at Huntly, in Aberdeenshire, on November 22nd, 1824.

Here is his own story of the great change: "On Thursday, 25th October, 1846, being the fast-day before communion, I attended Lady Glenorchy's church, where I heard Andrew Bonar, biographer of McCheyne, preach on the portion of the wicked in Psalm 11, 'Upon the wicked He shall rain snares, fire and brimstone, and an horrible tempest: this shall be the portion of their cup.' I felt as he proceeded as if all were to myself. I dreaded the portion I was about to receive. I knew I deserved it. I was standing on the 10th December, 1846, at the end of my father's house, and meditating on that precious word which has brought peace to countless weary ones: 'God so loved the world, that He gave His only begotten Son, that whosoever believeth in Him should not perish, but have everlasting life' (John 3. 16.) I saw that God loved me, for I was of the world. I saw the proof of His love in the giving of His Son, Jesus. I saw that 'whosoever' meant anybody and everybody, and therefore me, even me. I saw the result of believing—that I would not perish, but have everlasting life. I was enabled to take God at His word. I saw no one, but Jesus only, all in all in redemption. My burden fell from my back, and I was saved. "

Immediately on his conversion he began to labour for the salvation of souls. At first his light was small; but he kept trimming his lamp both for his own and others' good, and the flame increased. Every effort of faith and sacrifice of love seemed to add live coals to his altar of fire. For twenty years the flame of zeal was never suffered to expire; no, not for a single day. Night and day, in season and out of season, he strove with all his might to win souls.

His first attempt was at Burntisland, where the minister of the Free Church kindly gave him the use of the school, and otherwise encouraged him. He began by wisely conjoining the temporal with the spiritual, making the former subservient to the latter. Having acquired proficiency in drawing, he offered gratuitously to teach his fellow-workmen. The class was opened and closed with prayer and reading of the Word. His interest in the temporal well-being of the workmen was genuine; but he cared chiefly for their souls. While they were learning to draw sketches, he was striving to save sinners; while they studied architectural plans, he was brooding over plans for their salvation.

The Duchess of Gordon, hearing of young Matheson's zealous and successful labours, sent for him and offered to employ him as a missionary at a salary of forty pounds a year. Hitherto he had maintained himself: but his means were now exhausted. His worldly prospects were indeed bright. His skill as a builder, his energy, enterprising spirit, business talents, and moral integrity, held out the promise of position and wealth but he cheerfully turned his back on honour and gain, and betook himself amidst opposition and scorn to build the walls of Jerusalem.

Being now fully possessed by the great passion of his life, the saving of souls, worldly considerations were with him of small account. The offer of the Duchess was accepted. He went to work with all his might. Although he never received more than the small salary named, he spent a large proportion of it in the purchase of tracts, and in the relief of the poor; and this noble and generous practice he followed whilst he lived.

He frequently visited old Christians, and in his intercourse with them learned several useful lessons. One of these pilgrims was Isobel Chrystie, then upwards of ninety years of age. "Come awa, my son David," said Isobel to the missionary one day as he entered her humble cot. When in the course of conversation allusion was made to the salvation of the dying thief, she rattled her little staff on the floor and said, "That was a gey trophy to gang thro' the gowden gates o' Heaven. I'm thinkin' there was a gey steer amo' the angels; but nane o' them would try to pit him oot. Na, Na; Christ brocht him ben."

When Isobel lay dying she was unable to recognise minister, missionary, friend, or neighbour. To each enquiry she still replied, "I dinna ken you." At last the question was put to her, "Isobel, d'ye ken Christ?" The countenance of the dying saint brightened at the sound of her Saviour's name. Looking up with a smile she promptly replied, "That I do, but nae sae muckle as I would like, and will do by and by." That night the aged believer went to be with Him whom she remembered and knew when all others were forgotten and unknown.

The call which he was praying for came from an unexpected quarter, and it came stamped with the broad seal of a special providence. It happened in this way. One day he received a letter, which in substance ran thus: "If you are still in mind to go to the East, reply by return of post, and please say when you could start." The letter was from the Rev. J. Bonar, convener of the Colonial Committee of the Free Church—a gentleman whom Duncan Matheson had never seen, and did not know. Surely, he thought as he read Mr. Bonar's note, there is some mistake here. Yet he felt as if the hand and voice of God were in it, calling him to the scene of conflict.

He went and told the Duchess, saying that there was clearly a mistake, but that he was willing to go. "How strange!" exclaimed her Grace; "I have been praying that God would incline you to go, and others have been praying also. If there is a mistake, I will send you myself."

He wrote to Mr. Bonar and ascertained that the letter was intended for another of the same name, a Gaelic-speaking licentiate of the Free Church, who had been employed for some time among the navvies. The

Countess of Effingham, desirous of sending
a missionary to the Highland Brigade, had
requested Mr. Bonar to find a suitable agent
for the work. Mr. Bonar wrote to the Rev.
D. Matheson; but the letter going astray,
a clerk in the Post Office had written on it,
"Try Huntly, " and so it came into the hands
of the wrong D. Matheson, according to the
proposing of the man, but the right D. Matheson
according to the disposing of God.

Arrived in the Crimea, Matheson, with
characteristic generosity, immediately gave
away all the clothes he could spare, and
then began to distribute his spiritual stores
in the shape of tracts and Bibles, of which
latter there was a great scarcity in the camp.
The books, and especially the Bibles, were
received with the greatest eagerness. Some
25,000 tracts, selected by Peter Drummond,
of Stirling, and by Miss Marsh, were quickly
put into circulation.

He says he did not find many real Christians
in the army. There were a few stars of the
first magnitude, and they shone conspicuous
in so dark a sky. Our lay missionary was
not long in discovering those who feared the
Lord; and he found in them true friends. The
first time he entered the tent of Capt. Hedley
Vicars he observed that although the officer

was absent at the time, his Bible lay open upon a sort of table made of an old box. Thus the godly Vicars showed his colours, the open Bible intimating to all who entered on what terms they might have his fellowship. "His manliness and wholeheartedness," says Mr. Matheson, "struck you at once. There was nothing morose or gloomy about him; nothing to repel."

We give Matheson's account of what he accomplished in the Crimea:

"I hardly knew from what point to start to let you know of my work since entering this field of death and bloodshed. It has been an eventful, thrilling, soul-trying time; and yet in the midst of all, much of the seed of the kingdom has been scattered—seeing since 4th December last I have given away— tracts, 52,000; Bibles, 622; Testaments, 1477; French Testaments, 770; Bibles, 32; Italian Testaments, 4300; Bibles, 200; Welsh, Russian, and German Testaments, 173; books for officers, 450."

In October 1857, he went to labour as an evangelist in Whitehaven, at the request of a minister of the Church of England, who was desirous of promoting the spiritual welfare of his native place. He found the soil of Cumberland stiff; but his labours were not wholly in vain. It was a sowing time rather than a harvest. Then he began to preach every day, a practice he followed throughout the rest of his active ministry.

"To this place," he says in a letter, "I have almost done my duty. Surely if I go home I shall get a little rest. Rest did I say? Nay, truly, whilst health is granted. The days pass swiftly. Soon all will be gone. Since I came here I have not got half an hour to take my dinner at a time, and the door is widening on every hand."

Invited by Lady Pirrie, he went to Malvern in the autumn of 1858, and laboured there for a short time. Here on the hill-side he held his first open-air meeting, and felt he received a special call to this kind of work in the blessing that attended the service. Henceforth he gave himself to preaching in the open air. By day, by night, beneath the summer sun, out in the drenching rain or piercing cold of winter, in the remote glen amidst the bleating of the sheep, at the seaside, where the singing of David's psalms mingles with the still more ancient harmonies of the great ocean, on the crowded street, in the noisy fair, beneath the shadow of the scaffold, in the face of the raging mob— everywhere, in short, as far as in him lay,

he strove to preach Christ to perishing men.
In this way his voice reached many who otherwise would never have heard the glad tidings
of salvation.   He was one of the first to use
a bell in Gospel service.

From Malvern he retraced his steps to
Cumberland and for a while laboured at
Workington.   Here by invitation of the people
he occupied the pulpit of the Presbyterian
Church, and combined the offices of pastor
and evangelist.   His preaching excited no
ordinary interest.   Crowds flocked to hear
him, and not a few were impressed.

Towards the close of 1859 he began to extend
his evangelistic itineracy to Banffshire, preaching for the most part in the towns and villages
along the coast.   His labours were specially
blessed in the burgh and seaport of Cullen.
This little town is situated on the brow of
a hill looking full in the face at the blue waters
of the Northern Sea, where it begins to narrow
into the beautiful Firth of Moray, whose ample
tide is bounded on the southern shore by wild,
picturesque, and caverned rocks; whilst the
lofty mountains of Sutherland and Caithness
rise far across the deep, like giant warders
of the northern coast.   Beneath the burgh
proper lies the fishing village in a tumult
of houses upon the beach, where the storm

often breaks with Arctic fury, casting clouds of spray high into the air, and sometimes invading the cottages that line the shore.

Pushing along the coast as far north as Moray and Nairn, he bent his steps into the interior and visited Dufftown, Tomintoul, and Braemar. Sweeping southward to the counties of Forfar and Perth, he gradually extended his circuit until it embraced the whole country from John o' Groat's to the English border.

Castle Park. The first meetings here were held on the 25th and 26th July, 1860, and were renewed for three successive summers. Many thousands assembled year by year in the Castle Park, with its hoary ruins towering amid the softest scenes of sylvan beauty. Here of old the Gordon clan were wont to gather in preparation for some distant and bloody raid. Now another clan assembles for very different ends. The children of Zion gather themselves together to meet their King; the soldiers of the Cross rally around the standard of Christ. The coming and going of the people to serve God amidst the loveliest retreats of nature reminded one of the conventicles of the Covenanters in some remote glen or dewy hollow, and of the still more memorable scenes when multitudes gathered round the Prince of open-air preachers by the shores of the Sea of Galilee.

Here are extracts from Matheson's journal: "Forfar, September 10th, 1866. Praise the Lord, He has begun His work. We commenced on the street at seven on Saturday. A great crowd gathered round. They listened breathlessly. It was a blessed meeting. I have seldom seen such a solemn meeting on the streets. At eight we went to the school. A good company were present. At the close some waited in anxiety to be spoken with. We did not leave till ten.

"Yesterday Rice T. Hopkins, J. A. Boswell, and I, went through the streets giving tracts and speaking. We had solemn talks with the people. At six we met on the green. About one thousand were present. God helped us all wondrously. The people hung on our words. We then went to church. About four hundred came. It was a very solemn meeting. Rarely did I ever feel such a power at a meeting. About a hundred remained to the second meeting. Some ten or twelve were really anxious. We could hardly get the church cleared. An evangelist, who had been preaching in a village, came and had a meeting for the anxious in the street. Some one asked them in. He had to speak till eleven o'clock.

Some evidently found the Lord. Is it not blessed? I praise the Lord. The Lord send floods. It is sweet to see such fruit at first.

"September 13th. What a night we had last night! I shall never forget it. We met at one o'clock and spoke in a small street; at seven, Harrison Ord spoke at the Cross, and Hopkins and I took another place. We then collected all into a school. It was packed. At the close, on going out they laughed, swore, and mocked. Within we spoke to anxious souls, a few: and outside I tried to control the rabble. Oh, how obscene they were! It seemed as if the devil had entered into them. At ten o'clock we could hardly get the gate shut. We go to Mr. M'Phail's church to-night, as the school is too small. This is a fearful place. No tongue can tell its sin. I do pray that God may convert many. Nothing is too hard for Him. "

In person tall, erect, and broad-chested, with head firmly set upon the shoulders, and incapable of drooping, Duncan Matheson was the picture of manliness, self-reliance, and valour, while the main features of his countenance indicated, if we may believe physiognomy, the keenest discernment of human character. The glistening tear revealed the genuine tenderness of his heart, and the grace he displayed is marked by a severely plain monument on which is inscribed, as prepared by himself, the following epitaph:

> In Memory
> of
> DUNCAN MATHESON
> Editor 'Herald of Mercy,'
> and Evangelist.
> Born at Huntly, Nov. 22nd, 1824,
> Born again, Oct. 26th, 1846.
> Died Sept. 16th, 1869.
>
> 'And they that be wise shall shine as the brightness of the firmament: and they that turn many to righteousness as the stars for ever and ever' (Dan. xii. 3).

May the record of this earnest "chosen vessel" encourage all who read it to have a concern like him for the souls of men.

CHAPTER X

Lord Radstock

THE CONTINENTAL EVANGELIST

GRANVILLE AUGUSTUS WILLIAM WALDEGRAVE, was born on April 10th, 1833, the only son of the second Baron, Vice-Admiral Lord Radstock, C.B., and of Esther Caroline, his wife, the youngest daughter of John Puget of Totteridge, a Director of the Bank of England. His father, the Vice-Admiral, entered the Navy at the age of twelve, and saw much active service on the coast of Spain. Retiring in 1815, he devoted the remaining forty-two years of his life to the administration of naval charities.

His grandfather, the first Baron, was Admiral the Honourable William Waldegrave, G.C.B., second son of the third Earl Waldegrave. He had an active and successful career in the Navy, and his references to his friend Nelson, freely quoted by Mahan in his life of the hero, contain many illuminating comments on Nelson's character.

On his mother's side Lord Radstock was

descended from an old Huguenot family. His grandmother, Mrs. Catherine Puget of Totteridge, was a very remarkable woman of a fine type, and belonged to the old school of practical godliness. She was early left a widow with four children. Possessing great wealth, she bestowed her enormous charities over a very wide field, embracing Indian and Siberian Missions, French Protestants, German Lutherans, and the poor of London and of Ireland; she was also a benefactor of many needy curates, and of remote county parishes. She is found spending nights beside condemned criminals; and, attended by her faithful servant with a lantern, she traversed roads impassable at night by carriage, visiting distant hamlets and ministering to the sick and dying.

The nature of Lord Radstock was highly impetuous. He told how as a child, rushing headlong and falling, and as often rising again to pursue his wild career, he used to think of himself as some great prince with boundless power, and that he scarcely ever thought of himself except in this character, feeling that within his breast was a mighty secret unknown to those around. It was a parable and a forecast. In the mysterious purpose of God, some intimation seems often to exist in the mind of a child—an intimation that is worked out afterwards in the life, though it may be on a different plane.

It was after an accident at Harrow that he was asked, if he had died, whether he would have gone to Heaven or Hell. Realising that he was not good enough to go to Heaven, he still hoped he would not go to Hell. The efficacy of Christ, as a Saviour, then came into his mind and he thanked God for the wonderful mercy which availed him. Still he considered that "only just so much of the religious life need be added to his earthly life," with all its lower claims and ideals, as would secure his final salvation.

On leaving Baliol, after a life full of the usual interests and friendships—the school of Natural Science, Law and History, in which he took a Double Second; the cultivation of music to which he was devoted, society and sport—he went to the Crimea. Ere he arrived, the war came to an end, but on visiting the battle-fields he was stricken with fever, and no hope was given of his life. In his own words, "his last hour had come and he was not ready." But his cry for a reprieve was granted, and from that moment he realised the fact of a great and personal salvation.

In 1866 Lord Radstock felt he must give

up his whole life to making known this Gospel of a personal and immediate salvation. He therefore relinquished the command of the West Middlesex Volunteers in spite of the remonstrances of his friends, who deplored the influence which this step would forfeit. He answered by words often repeated in substance throughout his life when meeting with similar objections. "Human influence," he declared, "could not produce human results; what was needed was the power of the Holy Spirit without which even Apostles were powerless." This faithfulness was very shortly rewarded by a remarkable outpouring of the Holy Spirit upon his testimony at Weston-super-Mare, a fashionable watering-place where he had taken a house. The largest halls in the place were soon not large enough to contain the throngs who came to hear his words. Great was the new joy which many received making the former gaieties of the place lose their attraction. Balls and theatres were forsaken. If Dr. Bædeker had been the only result of Lord Radstock's mission to Weston, it would have been a rich reward for the renunciation of his military career. But that was not so; time would fail to tell of the illuminated lives, of the blessing of which after seventy years the results are still apparent.

The year 1867 marks a new epoch in Lord Radstock's life and an extension of his work. I quote from his notes. "I was asked," he says, "to take part in an International Conference of the Evangelical Alliance in Holland.

"I knew only one gentleman there; and the programme, which included many ponderous theological addresses by Dutch and German professors, was not attractive. But as it was a rallying point for Christians of all denominations, I went."

He proposed a daily prayer meeting before the Conference began, and in three or four days about four hundred met each morning at eight o'clock seeking blessing on Holland. Wonderful and speedy was the answer. At the Gospel Meetings which followed in the lovely villas and chateaux within reach of the Hague, great numbers of the educated classes were impressed.

In Belgravia he built the Conference Hall, Eccleston Street, at which he preached on Sunday afternoons for many years. His audiences were often small and to a great extent composed of the coachmen and servants in the neighbourhood, but there were some wonderful instances of blessing among them, for great truths were preached there, and great thoughts found expression.

There is an institution in Paris for which
an appeal is still made to-day.   It is a Home
for English Dancing Girls, and it was founded
and maintained by the late Lord Radstock.
It exists not to pluck them from the life of the
halls of Montmartre as brands from the burning,
but to afford them shelter from its dangers.
Lord Radstock was a Puritan of the Puritans,
and this instance of the extraordinary charity
of his nature is very striking.   Seven visits to
India, made between the years 1880 and 1910,
deserve more than a passing mention.   His
work here lay principally in addressing meetings
among the educated natives and in visiting
the Missions, cheering and sympathising with
the workers.   He was deeply interested in
and had an unusual affinity with the religious
aspirations and desires of the various Indian
races.

One deeply interesting result of one of his
later visits to India was the united gathering
in the largest hall of Calcutta of 1400 Christians,
English and native.   The meeting was by
ticket, and only those who professed and personally declared their faith in Christ were
admitted.   The Lieutenant-Governor of Bengal,
Sir Andrew Fraser, was present, and leading
members of the Council of India.   They all
united in the praise and worship of Christ,

recited together the Creed and sang in three
different languages, "All hail the power of
Jesu's Name." This meeting excited deep
interest in Calcutta, and was no doubt a
declaration of unity and very real sig-
nificance.

At another time, when living at Southsea,
he was awakened at three in the morning
by a strong impulse to dress and go out.
He at first tried to resist it, but so persistent
was it that in the cold winter morning he rose
and went out to the Common, where he found
a solitary man. That man in anguish of
soul had come out in his despair. God's
servant met him, and then and there light
dawned, and the burden rolled away.

His words at English watering-places came
as an alarum to the conventional upper classes
—classes so strangely free from care; rich,
with good traditions, yet still living for lower
aims and self satisfaction—and many received
new ideals of life and its glorious opportunities.
In Holland how different was the field, how
hard the ground of that reasoning, sceptical,
material society, encrusted within its ancient
pedigrees. His work was peculiar in its power
to reach those outside ordinary evangelistic
agencies, and through those possessed of influence and wealth his message penetrated to

the remotest parts of the country. The results which followed were strong and deep and a blessing to many.

In Paris the message was one of warning and forecast of coming judgment, while at the same time to the poor and oppressed was the Gospel preached.

Then came Russia, the most brilliant and satirical society in Europe, with charm and vivacity unequalled, with princely ideals, unconventional and unmoral; while under the surface, in the Slavonic nature lay passionate longings which could never be satisfied with material things.

In Scandinavia, amidst pure traditions and a high standard of education and general enlightenment, his message found awakened consciences, Bible knowledge, and simplicity of life to a remarkable degree; and this work in the Northern Peninsula had a character of its own, and his message a ready reception.

In the Latin countries visited in later life his witness was a different one. He spoke to many in the ecclesiastical and intellectual worlds of the true universality of the Church of God, far exceeding the boundaries of catholicity claimed by Rome.

Lord Radstock finished his earthly course in Paris, on December 8th, 1913.

CHAPTER XI

Dr. R. A. Torrey

THE WORLD-WIDE EVANGELIST

THE history of Christian progress is the history of men chosen of God. Every great movement of the church has been marked by activity in evangelism. The Great Reformation, marked by the work of Martin Luther and others who were called of God for special spiritual work during that definite period, was in a proper sense evangelistic. Later the Wesleys and John Knox followed the same trail. While they emphasised minor elements of the truth, they adhered closely to the message of the great evangel. Later still, D. L. Moody was called of God to push the battle to the gate in a series of stirring evangelistic campaigns.

The work of Mr. Moody was followed by that of a logical successor, Dr. REUBEN ARCHER TORREY, a man called of God for a special work at a special time. In every emergency in Christian work, God has always raised up His

servant to bring the message of salvation to a
lost and dying world. Regarded by some as
being unsuited to a specific evangelistic ministry, it cannot be denied that Dr. Torrey was
raised up for a great work. That he was called of
God is evidenced not only in his messages, but
in the abundant blessing attendant upon his
ministry. He had a brilliant career of study
at Hale, with further periods of study abroad.

His student days were marked by doubt,
and were threatened by disaster. It was then
he faced and fought some hard battles. At
one time it seemed certain he was doomed to
defeat. The young student was wavering. His
spiritual destiny was at stake, and some
Divine intervention was essential if his later
career was to be saved. At the time of the
most crucial test, young Torrey little realised
that his saintly mother at home was laying
siege on God in importunate prayer. The
crisis came, prayer prevailed, and the young
theological student emerged from the seclusion
of his room, battered by the storm, but victorious in a new-found faith.

He began his practical preparation for his
later work in a small pastorate in Ohio. It
was a community of several hundred people,
but even in this limited sphere the preacher
gave evidence of a definite call to the ministry.

He laboured incessantly, he preached faithfully, and he proved himself to be a real man of power, called to a definite work.

His call from God was proven by his spiritual equilibrium. While his soul soared to great spiritual heights as he meditated on the Word of God, this man kept both feet firmly planted on the ground. He was never fitful or spasmodic either in word or action, but possessed unusual balance in all his work and effort. Nor was he a man of moods.

He was endowed with an iron will which was tempered by his unchanging spiritual attitude. Such a will expressed itself readily in the rich and fertile soil of undiminished faith. The aggression of sin found him ever ready to exercise his conviction in a victorious attack. His will was God's will. Thus was his life victorious. He always faced an issue squarely and honestly. He was never sullen, but always acted in an upright straightforward way.

God was preparing this preacher for promotion, and as in all His purposes of grace, God uses human instrumentality. He was thus certain to use this method in dealing with His servant. The discipline of faith became a reality, as the work of the mission continued. Every answered prayer was a stimulus to greater trust, and the man of God exercised continued and increasing faith as time went on. To live this life meant renunciation, and called for whole-souled devotion to Christ.

And then, one day, his training and testing in the life of faith being well advanced, the opportunity of a larger field of service presented itself. God put it into the heart of D. L. Moody to call His servant to Chicago. It was a sudden call and quite unexpected. Once again God in His infinite wisdom brought the unexpected things to pass. Mr. Moody was endowed with a keen insight into the character of men, such as few of his fellows possessed. The work in Chicago required the services of a man of tried and proved faith. Mr. Moody was convinced that he had found that man in Reuben Archer Torrey.

At one Saturday night prayer meeting, Dr. Torrey was suddenly led to pray that God would send him around the world preaching the Gospel, and that he might see thousands of conversions in China, Japan, Australia, New Zealand, Tasmania, India, England, Scotland, Ireland, Germany, and America. He mentioned all these countries in his prayer. The prayer was not his own. He was quite outside himself as he prayed borne along by the Holy Spirit. The others present united heartily in this petition with much assurance that it would be granted.

Shortly after this, two strangers appeared in the lecture room of the Moody Bible Institute day after day. Not much notice was taken of them, since one was the father of a student in the Institute. One day these two men spoke to Dr. Torrey at the close of a lecture and asked for a private interview. When they came to his office, they said: "When we left Australia, we were commissioned to visit Keswick and other centres in England and America and to select someone to invite him for a series of Evangelistic meetings in Australia. We have been at Keswick and elsewhere, and both of us have decided that you are the man to invite. Will you go?" Dr. Torrey gave an attentive hearing. His reply at first disappointed the two Christian envoys, inasmuch as it suggested the impossibility of leaving the Church and the Bible Institute. "I shall pray about the matter, and leave it to God to decide, " came the final answer.

As might be expected, this man of God, a man of faith and prayer, was also a man of strong conviction. Of his many outstanding Christian qualities, his unalterable conviction regarding the reality of God, the truth of the Word of God, and the undeniable right of every true believer in the matter of prayer, stands as one of the strongest. It mattered not to him what others did, he was always impelled, both in speech and action, by an unshaken conviction.

This conviction was not born in a day. It matured through the years, and developed to such a point that, in his public utterances, every word was stamped by the trade mark of proven conviction. He was not a man of caprice. His mental strength made that impossible, and this training, both in university and by experience, only served to reinforce his natural trend. The opinions of man were of little importance to him. He fought his own intellectual and spiritual battles single handed. He arrived at his acceptance of the Bible as the Word of God through a process of logical reasoning. In all his decisions he sought a higher source of approval than that of any mere man. His theological position was not merely positive; it was absolutely dogmatic. Never was he swayed by the innumerable passing religions, fads, and fancies of the day. This man built not upon the sand, but rather reared an impregnable fortress of faith on the solid foundation of a deeply-rooted conviction that the Bible was the Word of God. His yea was yea, and his nay, nay.

One instance comes forcibly to mind in this connection. The city of Sydney, Australia, a city of over one million inhabitants, was being shaken by the power of the preached word. The great town hall was overcrowded each night with thousands of people. Noonday meetings for business men were held in a large auditorium in the heart of the business district. In one of his addresses dealing with the crucifixion of our Lord, Dr. Torrey said, "The Unitarians of Christ's day crucified Christ." It was a startling statement, and at once aroused the ire of a certain element in the city. Controversy raged, and the discussion advertised the campaign as nothing else could.

Within a day or two, a local Unitarian pastor, together with his official board, published in the daily press a challenge calling on Dr. Torrey to either prove the charge or withdraw it. Interest in the campaign was thus fostered in a remarkable way. The noonday meetings were crowded an hour before the scheduled time, and at one of these gatherings, Dr. Torrey announced that on the following day he would answer the challenge. A special invitation was extended to the Unitarian pastor and his official board to occupy the front row of seats on the floor of the auditorium. The invitation was accepted, and, on the appointed day, the pastor occupied the centre seat, surrounded by a dozen of his church officers. He was a man of striking appearance, tall, clean shaven, with a decided intellectual bearing. In any company he would be an unusual figure.

The great auditorium was packed to the limit. The air was tense, and there was expectation of dramatic happenings. What would Dr. Torrey do? Would he withdraw his statement? Would he prove his charge? Such were the questions and whisperings among the audience. In his usual dignified manner he walked to the platform. There was little singing that day.

Very soon the speaker arose. "I have a request to-day," said he. "It comes from a certain Unitarian pastor of this city (giving his name). This preacher asks for the privilege of using this platform to answer a statement I made here a few days ago. That statement was to this effect, 'The Unitarians of Christ's day crucified Christ.' My conviction in this matter is based on the historic account of the crucifixion of our Lord." One could hear a pin drop, such was the absolute quiet of the huge audience. "But," Dr. Torrey continued, "before I can allow this man to share this platform with me, I must make sure that his record is clean. I hold in my hand the record of a certain pastor, bearing the same name as this preacher, who directed the affairs of a Unitarian Church in Boston, Massachusetts. He abandoned his wife, and later went to New Zealand with another man's wife. He then moved to Tasmania, only to be driven from that island by an infuriated mob. He then moved to this city, and became pastor of a Unitarian Church. Until I am assured that this preacher is not that man, I cannot allow him to speak from this platform."

The audience broke into prolonged applause. The Unitarian pastor and his colleagues looked at one another as if seeking some denial of this statement, but no denial was forthcoming, and Dr. Torrey was left in triumphant possession.

The Royal Albert Hall, London, was taxed to its utmost capacity with a great surging throng of people. The arena, the tiers of private boxes, the gallery and the capacious balcony were all crowded with a varied, interesting audience. The attraction was no great operatic or world-famed concert artist. It was one of a lengthy series of evangelistic services, in which the simple, unadulterated Gospel of the Lord Jesus Christ was being proclaimed.

The sermon was preached from the text,
"The hail shall sweep away the refuge of
lies" (Isa. 28. 17). It was an oft repeated
sermon, but the power was ever the same.
Stolid Englishmen listened, some with critical
ears, others more sympathetically. The invitation for decision for Christ was given. It was
always given in the same identical language.
For a few moments there was silence. No one
moved. The invitation was repeated as everybody sat up. No heads were lowered. Soon
a man arose. "God bless you; remain standing," said the preacher. Others took courage
and stood until over three hundred men and
women were on their feet. "Step to the
front!" It was a command rather than a
request. And they came. Conviction of sin
was evidenced. They were all personally
dealt with by trained workers. Later they
arose and made public confession of Christ.
It was a service of remarkable power.

The hands of Dr. Torrey were never tainted
with the stain of ill-gotten gains. His conscience was never seared by the blight of
sinful folly in the pursuit of doubtful notoriety.
His mind was never obscured by the cloud
of pretence in any form. His heart was never
divided in its devotion to God. He elevated
evangelism in every detail of his work. He

raised its standard to a lofty pinnacle by his unselfish attitude and unstinted service. This faithful preacher of the Gospel has vindicated sane evangelism. He has proven its eternal value. He has confirmed its worth to the Kingdom of God.

His name is fragrant throughout the whole world to-day, and will long continue to be so wherever the Gospel is preached in sincerity and truth.

CHAPTER XII

William Booth

THE FIRE-BRAND EVANGELIST

WILLIAM BOOTH was born in Nottingham on 10th April, 1829. In 1844 he experienced the great change of conversion, regarding which he wrote, "I felt that I could willingly and joyfully travel to the ends of the earth for Jesus Christ, and suffer anything imaginable to help the souls of other men."

He soon began to engage in Christian service, and made himself an apostle to the lads of Nottingham slums. He preached to them in the open, gathered a circle about him, and was on fire to bring them within the fold of the Methodists. If he was happy kneeling in the streets at night and praying with them, he desired to be happier still by praying with them on Sunday, praying within the walls of Wesley Chapel.

Later he arrived in London as a seeker of work, the son of a poor and struggling mother in the provinces, with no influence, with no money, and with no friends. For some time, strangely enough, he worked in a pawnbroker's shop in Walorth, but the more he saw of London, the more insistent became his desire to preach Christ. The spectacle of the London streets, thronged at nights by crowds of people who often appeared before his vision as godless, vicious, and perishing, worked upon his imagination and quickened the idea that he should preach Christ, whatever might be the consequences to his earthly fortunes.

To William Booth the call to preach Christ came in these London streets, not dramatically and suddenly, but with a steady and persisting tone of resolute command. He could rot doubt the reality of that call, and his faith would not let him disobey it.

E. J. Rabbits, a Wesleyan layman, who was among the reformers, was thus enabled to prevail on William Booth to leave his situation, and devote his time to preaching, undertaking to pay him a weekly wage for a period of three months. Various formative experiences began to manifest themselves in the life of William Booth about this time. He fell in love with his future wife. That had a determining effect upon his character and service. In course of time we find William

Booth preaching in Lincolnshire among the Methodists.

God owned the labours of His servant in the salvation of souls, and in the stirring up of the people. But he was a sort of fire brand, and the authorities of the Methodists were not attracted to the methods of such a one. Accordingly a historic point is reached at the Connexion Conference held on the Tyneside. The following extract is worthy of insertion here: "It is sufficient to say that this Conference was held in a chapel and that Mrs. Booth, who was seated with other members of the public in the gallery, when questioned by a glance from her husband in the pews below as to whether he should accept a miserable compromise, rose in her place and exclaimed in a determined voice, which startled the business-like gentlemen below, 'Never!' At that resolute exclamation Mr. Booth, we are told, sprang to his feet, and bowing to the chair, 'waved his hat in the direction of the door.' Amidst shouts of 'order, order,' he passed down the chapel, met his wife at the foot of the gallery stairs, embraced her, and went out to face the consequences of his act." After seven years of devoted service, he was penniless; and this time he had a wife and children for whom he and no other could provide.

The evangelist's fire was in his bones so off to Cornwall he went, and despite the opposi- of the churches, many souls were gathered in. From there he went to Cardiff, and experienced times of blessing.

To Whitechapel he comes, and there starts preaching. Listen to his words, "I saw multitudes of my fellow-creatures not only without God and hope but sunk in the most desperate forms of wickedness and misery that can be conceived. I went out and looked on the wretched sons and daughters of debauchery and vice and crime, who were all about me. The drunkenness, and harlotry, and pauperism, and slumdom, and blasphemy, and infidelity of these crowds had a fascination for me. I not only saw but compassionated the people sunk in the sin and wretchedness that I beheld, and the everlasting woe that I knew must follow."

At length his "Christian Mission" was transformed into "The Salvation Army," when William Booth had entered on his fiftieth year, and he became "General" Booth. The pathway was not a smooth one. He was criticised and persecuted; oftentimes negotiations were in progress to bring him and his work into close association with the Church of England; while all the time he was forging ahead and rallying round him a band of workers, whom he was always urging to "do something!"

Late one night—it was in the early morning hours—in the year 1888 William Booth returned home from a campaign in the south of England, and felt exceedingly ill when he arrived at his house. Bramwell Booth, living near by, was early in attendance next morning, and scarcely had he entered the dressing room, quick, alert, and cheerful, when his father, who was walking to and fro with hanging braces and tousled hair, burst out at him, "Here, Bramwell! do you know that fellows are sleeping out at night on the bridges? Sleeping out all night on the Viaduct?" Bramwell, thus checked in his greeting, exclaimed, "Yes, General; why? didn't you know that!" The General appeared to be thunderstruck. He had seen those tragic huddled forms benched on stone for the first time on the previous night, and his own sleep in a warm bed had been robbed in consequence. "You knew that," he said, "and you haven't done anything!" Thus began the social work of the Salvation Army.

For a number of years William Booth travelled in all parts of the world in the interests of his great work. He interviewed some of the greatest men of the day. And yet, wherever he went, he endeavoured to establish contact with men of all classes regarding there spiritual welfare.

Towards the close of his life evidences are not lacking that he desired to lay greater stress on the Gospel side of his work rather than the social. Note this, "We were packed last night at the social lecture, and had a pretty good time, although I must say I am heartily tired of social schemes in places where I can get a crowd, and get souls saved." Another extract—"I thought again as I was speaking last night that nearly all the things I said cut into the hearts of the people, and the incidents I produced for their wondering amazement, were the result of Blood-and-Fire Salvation, that is the hook that lands the fish."

William Booth was a man who saw the great and crying needs of his fellow-men and believed that the one and only remedy was to be found in the Gospel. He was loyally supported by his wife who was possessed of considerable spiritual insight. He loved his children, and was desirous for their well-being in the things of God. He was handicapped by physical weakness, but his indomitable spirit enabled him to go on in spite of difficulties.

He seldom knew a leisure moment. He had been welcomed by kings, presidents, and rulers, and near the end wondered if he "had gone down to Egypt for too much help." When he was "promoted to Glory," his name and work commanded the respect and sympathy of all classes of men and women in the world.

It was an experience which left an abiding impression on a young man to listen to this veteran speaking for one hour and a half, during which time he sustained the interest of a large audience, and then to see his tall, lean, and venerable figure lead the congregation in the singing of "When I survey the wondrous Cross." Verily, as we have seen in passing through the pages of this little picture gallery, there are diversities of gifts. May we seek likewise to use "the gift" which undoubtedy God has given to us.